JAMES
BECKWOURTH

MOUNTAINEER, SCOUT, AND PIONEER

SPECIAL LIVES IN HISTORY THAT BECOME

Signature LIVES

JAMES
BECKWOURTH
MOUNTAINEER, SCOUT, AND PIONEER

By Susan R. Gregson

Content Adviser: Dr. David Smith,
Adjunct Assistant Professor of History,
University of Michigan, Ann Arbor

Reading Adviser: Rosemary G. Palmer, Ph.D.,
Department of Literacy, College of Education,
Boise State University

COMPASS POINT BOOKS MINNEAPOLIS, MINNESOTA

Compass Point Books
3109 West 50th Street, #115
Minneapolis, MN 55410

Visit Compass Point Books on the Internet at *www.compasspointbooks.com*
or e-mail your request to *custserv@compasspointbooks.com*

Editor: Editorial Directions, Inc.
Lead Designer: Jaime Martens
Photo Researcher: Marcie C. Spence
Page Production: The Design Lab, Bobbie Nuytten
Cartographer: XNR Productions, Inc.
Educational Consultant: Diane Smolinski

Managing Editor: Catherine Neitge
Creative Director: Keith Griffin
Editorial Director: Carol Jones

Library of Congress Cataloging-in-Publication Data
Gregson, Susan R.
   James Beckwourth : mountaineer, scout and pioneer / by Susan R. Gregson.
      p. cm.—(Signature lives)
   Includes bibliographical references (p.   ) and index.
   ISBN 0-7565-1000-7 (hardcover)
   1. Beckwourth, James Pierson, 1798–1866—Juvenile literature.
2. African American pioneers—West (U.S.)—Biography—Juvenile
literature. 3. African American trappers—West (U.S.)—Biography—
Juvenile literature. 4. Pioneers—West (U.S.)—Biography—Juvenile
literature. 5. Trappers—West (U.S.)—Biography—Juvenile literature.
6. Frontier and pioneer life—West (U.S.)—Juvenile literature. 7. West
(U.S.)—Biography—Juvenile literature. I. Title. II. Series.
   F592.B393G74 2006
   978'.02'092--dc22   2005003258

AMERICAN FRONTIER ERA

By the late 1700s, the United States was growing into a nation of homesteaders, politicians, mountain men, and American dreams. Manifest Destiny propelled settlers to push west, conquering and "civilizing" from coast to coast. In keeping with this vision, world leaders hammered out historic agreements such as the Louisiana Purchase, which drastically increased U.S. territory. This ambition often led to bitter conflicts with Native Americans trying to protect their way of life and their traditional lands. Life on the frontier was often filled with danger and difficulties. The people who wove their way into American history overcame these challenges with a courage and conviction that defined an era and shaped a nation.

Table of Contents

1 FRIEND OR FOE?

ᘓᕽᘔᕽ

The Crow called him Morning Star, Bloody Arm, and Enemy of Horses. The Sac knew him as Dark Sky. To the Cheyenne, he was known as Medicine Calf. Each tribe he met gave him a different name based on his appearance, his skills as a warrior, or his role in their tribe. His real name was James Pierson Beckwourth, one of the first African-Americans to head West. For 50 years, Indians on the Great Plains and in the Rocky Mountains considered him a friend. Then, in one tragic event, he became the enemy.

In 1864, in Denver, Colorado, tensions ran deep between white settlers and their Indian neighbors. A few scattered Indian attacks on white residents threatened the safety of Denver's citizens. One man in particular spoke out with particular hatred for the

James Beckwourth was admired and accepted by several Indian tribes.

Indians: Colonel John M. Chivington, a Methodist minister and career military man.

Unlike Beckwourth, Chivington spurned the idea of making peace with the Cheyenne. He said, "It is simply not possible for Indians to obey or even understand any treaty. I am fully satisfied, gentlemen, that to kill them is the only way we will ever have peace and quiet in Colorado." Chivington looked at events from the white man's point of view. He had conveniently forgotten that treaties with the Indians were usually broken by the whites. He ignored the history of whites attacking natives, stealing their land, and mistreating Indian women and children.

A few scattered Indian raids in Colorado led to tensions there in 1864.

Chivington developed an Indian-removal action plan. He would lead a regiment of Colorado volun-

teers, together with cavalry troops from Fort Lyon, in an attack against the Cheyenne and Arapaho camped at Sand Creek. The cavalry's leader, Major Scott J. Anthony, looked forward to a bit of slaughter and gladly agreed to join Chivington.

In November 1864, Chivington's troops surrounded Fort Lyon. No one could leave. This measure ensured that the Cheyenne would not find out about the attack in advance.

A smaller troop surrounded William Bent's ranch. Bent was married to a Cheyenne woman and had three sons, George, Robert, and Charlie. Two of them were camped with the Cheyenne. Chivington thought Bent would warn the Cheyenne, so he placed Bent in custody. Right before Chivington arrived at Fort Lyon, Major Anthony suggested that the Cheyenne braves leave to hunt buffalo about 50 miles (80 kilometers) to the east. With most of the tribe's warriors gone, the remaining Indians were easy pickings.

Chivington could hardly wait for the massacre. He was thrilled at the idea of scalping and mutilating the Cheyenne and Arapaho, who were sharing their winter camp. Not all the officers agreed with Chivington's plan. Captain Silas Soule and Lieutenants Joseph Cramer and James Connor called the plan a cowardly act of murder.

Their opinions angered Chivington. He yelled, "Damn any man who sympathized with Indians! I

*Black Kettle (?–1868),
a southern Cheyenne
chief, worked to gain
peace with honor for his
people. His tribe lived
in Indian Territory in
western Kansas and
eastern Colorado. As
white settlers moved
into the area, the U.S.
government forced the
Cheyenne to live on
barren land in Colorado
called the Sand Creek
Reservation. Black
Kettle escaped the
slaughter at Sand
Creek. Four years later,
George Armstrong
Custer killed Black
Kettle while the chief
was living on a
Cheyenne reservation.*

have come to kill Indians, and believe it is right and honorable to use any means under God's heaven to kill Indians."

The troops needed a guide to lead them to the Cheyenne's camp. Chivington chose James Beckwourth, a man in his 60s who had lived among the Cheyenne and knew their ways. He had spent most of his adult life among the Crow, Cheyenne, and Blackfoot Indians.

By this time, Beckwourth was an old man and suffered the aches and pains of age. His eyesight was failing; his bones creaked. And he wasn't keen on helping Chivington.

But Chivington gave Beckwourth no choice. He could either serve as a guide or be hanged.

Seven hundred men moved out of Fort Lyon at night on November 28, 1864. Beckwourth rode by Chivington's side. Many of the troops were poorly trained volunteers. Some drank whiskey as they rode through the chilly night. The band did not have the skills or discipline of an "all-Army" troop.

As dawn broke the following morning, the

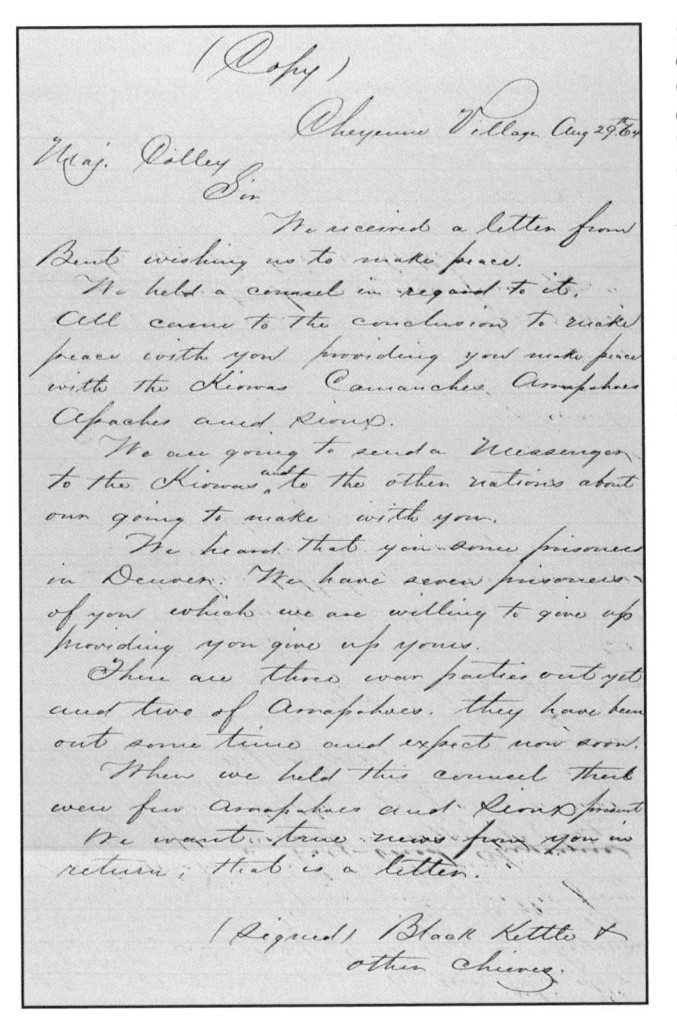

(Copy)

Cheyenne Village Aug 29 64

Maj. Colley
Sir

We received a letter from Bent wishing us to make peace. We held a council in regard to it. All came to the conclusion to make peace with you providing you make peace with the Kiowas Camanches Arrapahoes Apaches and Sioux.

We are going to send a Messenger to the Kiowas and to the other nations about our going to make with you.

We heard that you some prisoners in Denver. We have seven prisoners of yours which we are willing to give up providing you give up yours.

There are three war parties out yet and two of Arrapahoes. they have been out some time and expect now soon.

When we held this council there were few Arrapahoes and Sioux present. We want true news from you in return; that is a letter.

(Signed) Black Kettle & other Chiefs.

The Cheyenne camped at Sand Creek hoped to avoid conflict with white settlers. In August 1864, George Bent copied a letter dictated by Chief Black Kettle to the Army. In this letter, Black Kettle expressed his desire for peace.

Cheyenne and Arapaho camp woke to the thunder of hoofbeats. Chief Black Kettle came out of his tepee and stood by the American flag. He had been told by U.S. Army officers that the flag would offer protection for the tribe. George Bent, one of William Bent's sons who witnessed the massacre, said, "I heard him [Black Kettle] call to the people not to be afraid, that the soldiers would not hurt them; then the troops opened fire from two sides of the camp." Bullets flew. Bodies fell. Indian blood painted the earth a dull reddish-brown. Old men, women, children, infants in their mothers' arms ... no one was safe. The soldiers shot the Cheyenne and Arapaho as they ran for cover.

Robert, another of William Bent's sons, later described the sight with disgust:

> *I saw one squaw lying on the bank whose leg had been broken by a shell; a soldier came up to her with a drawn saber; she raised her arm to protect herself, when he struck, breaking her arm. ... I saw a little girl of about five years of age who had been hid in the sand; two soldiers discovered her, drew their pistols and shot her. ... I saw quite a number of infants in arms killed with their mothers.*

Some Cheyenne and Arapaho managed to escape. Beckwourth saved William Bent's third son, Charlie, by hiding the lad in a wagon carrying a wounded Army officer. He later handed Charlie over to his brother Robert. The surviving Indians faced a 50-mile (80-km) journey east to the hunting camp. They walked hour after hour, shocked by the morning's massacre. The weather turned so cold that their bleeding wounds froze. The Cheyenne and Arapaho survivors had no food or blankets, no weapons with which to hunt. They barely escaped with their lives.

Chivington boasted of his success in the massacre at Sand Creek. He claimed to have killed 400 braves, but his numbers were exaggerated. In truth, 105 Indian women and children had been murdered in cold blood, their heads scalped, and their bodies mutilated. Only 28 Indian men died in the slaughter, and most of them were elderly. Nine of Chivington's men were killed, and 38 were wounded. Ironically, most of the wounded soldiers had been shot by their fellow troops, who were either drunk or had such poor aim that they hit their own men.

After the massacre, Indian tribes that had once fought each other banded together and smoked the war pipe. Arapaho, Sioux, and Cheyenne warriors

Arapaho, Sioux, and Cheyenne Indians responded to the Sand Creek Massacre by raiding wagon trains and attacking white settlers.

James Beckwourth was not the only African-American to head West. Clara Brown, born a slave in Tennessee, was the first African-American woman to cross the Plains and reach the Colorado gold fields. "Stagecoach" Mary Fields traveled with Mother Amadeus to start a school for the Blackfoot tribe in Montana. Escaped slave Ned Huddleston teamed up with Mexican bandits and smuggled stolen horses across the Rio Grande. Nat "Deadeye Dick" Love was a champion roper, crack shot, and broncobuster.

became brothers in the battle for revenge. They wanted to spill the white man's blood, just as the white man spilled Indian blood during the revolting slaughter of Cheyenne and Arapaho women and children. War parties began raiding wagon trains, killing settlers, and even burning whole villages.

The government realized that Chivington's solution to the Indian problem simply created a bigger dilemma. They sent Beckwourth to seek peace with the Cheyenne. He entered the lodge of the new chief, Leg-in-the-Water. The chief asked him why he had come. Was he bringing more soldiers to kill Cheyenne women and children?

I told them I had come to persuade them to make peace with the whites, as there was not enough of them to fight the whites. ... "We know it," was the general response of the council. "But what do we want to live for? The white man has taken our country, killed all of our game; was not satisfied with that, but killed our wives and children ... We have raised the battle ax until death."

Beckwourth was born a slave on a Virginia plantation.

The Cheyenne council told Beckwourth to leave, to return to the whites. He was no longer a brother to the Cheyenne. Fifty years of friendship disappeared with one tragic event.

But what about those 50 years? How had James Pierson Beckwourth lived? He was born a slave in Virginia and moved to Missouri as a child. He was a trapper and trader, mountain man and Indian war chief. He developed a reputation as a crack shot, a brave fighter, and a talented liar. What kind of childhood and life experiences led Beckwourth to earn his notorious reputation?

2 CHILD OF THE WILD

❧

Virginia plantation life was comfort and ease for the owners, but hard work and hardship for the workers. In the western part of Virginia (modern-day West Virginia) in about 1800, those workers were usually African slaves. Plantation owners lived in large houses, ate fine meals, and wore the best clothing tailors could provide. The master owned acres of land, horses, cattle, and people—slaves. In the young state of Virginia, slaves were property and could be bought or sold. The slaves lived in rough huts, survived on meager rations, and had one set of clothes. Overseers forced them to work by laying a whip to their skin.

Many masters had children by slave women. Like their mothers, these children were destined to

African slaves were treated like property and sold at auctions.

By the mid-1800s, slavery divided the nation into North and South. The North, a growing industrial center, wanted slavery ended. The South, an agricultural economy, felt it needed slave labor to survive. In 1861, Southern forces opened fire on Fort Sumter in Charleston, South Carolina. Southern states left the United States of America and formed the Confederate States of America. Slavery legally ended in the South when President Abraham Lincoln issued the Emancipation Proclamation in 1863. But the Civil War was still raging at that time, and Southerners refused to free their slaves until the conflict officially ended in 1865.

work in fields or elegant plantation homes. Few plantation owners acknowledged their slave sons and daughters. Their slave children plowed fields and picked cotton beside their African brothers and sisters. But James Pierson Beckwourth, the half-black son of a plantation owner, enjoyed a different destiny and ultimately followed an unusual path for a man born into slavery.

James was born in about 1800 in Frederick County, Virginia. His father, a wealthy landowner, was Jennings Beckwith. James' mother was probably Beckwith's slave. Her name and background are unknown. (James' last name was changed to Beckwourth in 1856 when his autobiography, *The Life and Adventures of James P. Beckwourth, Mountaineer, Scout, Pioneer*, and *Chief of the Crow Nation*, was published. The editor made a mistake.)

Sir Jennings came from a prominent Virginia family that traced its ancestors back to English

nobility. At 19, he served as a captain in the Revolutionary War. He later married a woman named Catherine Miskell in 1787. Catherine died sometime before 1800, the year James was born. After Catherine's death, James' mother and Jennings lived together as a husband and wife. In his autobiography, James wrote, "My father's family consisted of thirteen children, seven sons and six daughters ... I was the third child." Outside of this comment, few records of Beckwourth's family exist.

In the early 1800s, Virginia was a slave state. Slavery provided a cheap labor force for the growing agriculture-based economy. Wealth lay in the hands of a few plantation owners. Plantation farming gen-

Jennings Beckwith served as a captain in the Revolutionary War.

erally revolved around one of three basic crops—tobacco, cotton, or indigo. Plantation owners were self-sufficient, growing their own food, milling lumber, and raising and harvesting crops. The more slaves a plantation owner kept, the more work could be done on the plantation. Virginia's white society saw nothing wrong with owning blacks.

Since his mother was a slave, James was considered a slave, too. But historians believe that Jennings Beckwith did not treat James or his brothers and sisters as slaves. They lived in his home, learned to read and write, and ate at the Beckwith dinner table.

Most people in Virginia didn't agree with Beckwith's attitude toward his half-black children. It was all right to father slave children. It was completely wrong to love them. Accepted social ideas made it difficult for the Beckwiths to live openly as a family. But Jennings Beckwith didn't care. He loved his children, and the wagging tongues of Virginia's society did not change him. He had no interest in being socially acceptable.

Although Jennings Beckwith doted on his children, they still had to work. Chores on an early 19th-century plantation consumed all waking hours. James' mother cooked over a wood-burning stove. She cleaned rugs by pounding the dust and dirt out. The family wore clothes she stitched by hand. A typical day began before dawn and involved stoking up the fire and baking before the heat of the sun made the kitchen unbearable. It ended with darning socks or repairing clothes by candlelight.

James and his siblings had their share of chores. They helped with cooking, cleaning, chopping wood, hauling water from the pump, and tending the kitchen garden. When there was time to relax, the family might have danced, sung, played games such as marbles, or told stories.

In 1800, Frederick County included 12 present-day counties, seven of which are now in West Virginia. Crude dirt roads connected farms and small communities to larger cities that had shops, taverns, and smithies. A trip to the city was a treat

Life on a Virginia plantation was filled with hard work that lasted from before dawn until after dusk.

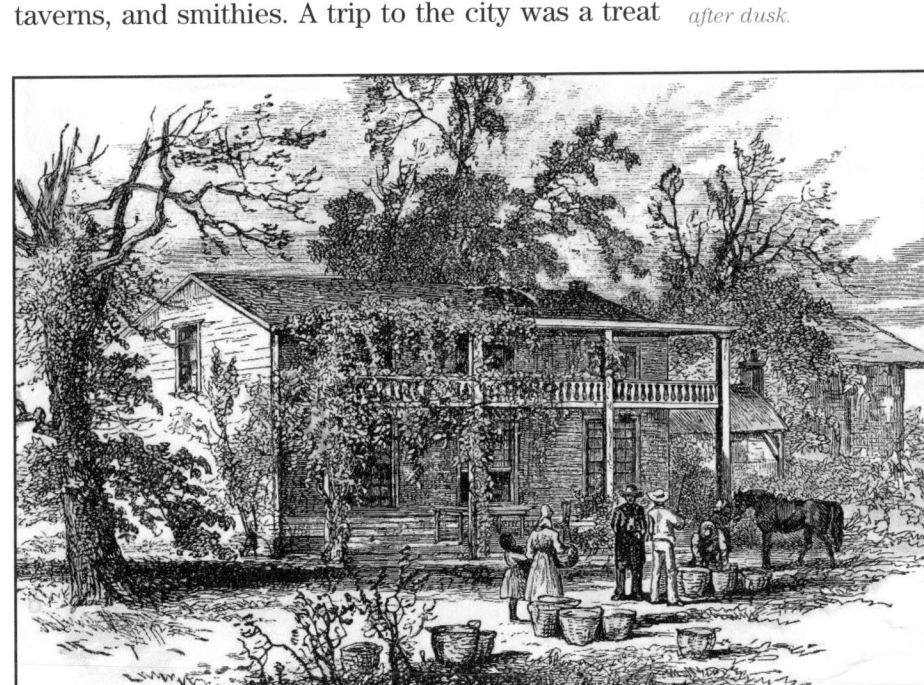

despite the rough wagon ride to get there. If nothing else, it was a day away from household chores. Even though the Beckwiths may not have lived in a big city, they did not lead isolated lives. Neighbors called to visit. Church drew friends together each Sunday. And Jennings Beckwith maintained friendships with men who served with him in the Army. James recalled these men coming to the house to sit with his father and tell stories of the Revolutionary War:

> *I well recollect, when a small boy, the frequent meetings of the old patriots at my father's house, who would sit down and relate the different battles in which they had taken part during those "days that tried men's souls." Often during these reminiscences every eye would dim and tears course down the cheeks of the old veterans, as they thus fought their battles o'er again.*

In 1808, James' family and 22 blacks from the plantation moved to land near St. Charles, Missouri. St. Charles was a growing town where settlers mingled with local Indian tribes and traded alcohol, beads, blankets, guns, and ammunition for beaver pelts. The pelts were worth a great deal of money. In Europe, beaver hats were popular fashion accessories of the day. The demand for pelts created a healthy fur trade with the Indians.

St. Charles had been the first permanent white settlement on the Missouri River and one of the first stops on the historic Lewis and Clark expedition four years earlier. In 1804, William Clark wrote: "a number Spectators french & Indians flocked to the bank to See the party. This Village is about one mile in length, Situated on the North Side of the Missourie ... those people appear Pore, polite & harmonious."

Beckwith acquired nearly 1,300 acres (520 hectares) of land between the Mississippi and Missouri rivers in an area called The Point. Historians believe Beckwith moved his family to the edge of America's "howling wilderness" so that he, James' mother, their children, and their friends could enjoy each other without the bigotry and social pressures that opposed blacks and whites living together in Virginia.

In addition to his desire to live more openly with his family, Beckwith also loved life on the edge of the frontier. He enjoyed fishing the

In 1803, President Thomas Jefferson more than doubled the size of the United States. He bought the Louisiana Territory from France. Meriwether Lewis and William Clark set off to explore and map the new land in 1804. They were to find the source of the Missouri River, reach the Pacific Ocean by traveling overland, and report on the Indians they met along the way. Their journey took them into land that no white men had ever seen before. They met and befriended many Indian tribes, saw animals unknown to science, and mapped their trip through the Rocky Mountains. The men recorded the details of their journey in a daily journal.

Beckwith saw Missouri as an opportunity to live openly with his family.

streams of the northern Ozark Mountains. He hunted game with his friends and local Indians.

Missouri was truly the gateway to the West. Along its eastern border, the Mississippi River carved its way northward. The Missouri River led to the Great Plains and waving seas of grass. But territorial life, while exciting, also carried its share of hard work and hazards. Land had to be cleared and prepared for planting. A house had to be built. And, of course, there was always hunting and cooking, cleaning, piles of laundry, and endless household chores.

A frontier wife's day began at 4:30 A.M. Once out of bed, she lit the fire, swept the floor, and cooked breakfast while her husband milked the cows. She fed the pigs, turned the cows into the pasture, made the beds, and cleaned the parlor—all by 7 A.M. The rest of the day included feeding and dressing the children, hoeing the garden, churning butter, doing the afternoon milking, and killing and plucking a chicken for dinner. One frontier woman said:

> *By this time it is 8 o'clock P.M.; my husband has come home, and we are eating supper; when we are through eating I make the beds ready, and the children and their father go to bed, and I wash the dishes and get things in shape to get breakfast quickly next morning. It is now about 9 o'clock P.M., and after a short prayer I retire for the night.*

The Beckwith's log house was probably one large room with a single window and a chimney— the standard family cabin for Missouri. After a day's hunting, Jennings Beckwith likely hung his rifle above the hearth. A deerskin served as a rug by the fireplace. James' mother cooked meals over an open fire, and bread baked in ovens built into the fireplace. Beans and biscuits, venison stew, and grilled fish regularly appeared on the family menu.

Rough wooden shelves held pots and pans,

plates and mugs, utensils, and the family's books. Trunks replaced closets for storing the Beckwiths' clothes, blankets, and linens.

Frontier families gathered for breakfast and supper around a large wooden table that stood in the center of the room. Frontier men usually ate a noon meal in the fields or forests. As they had in Virginia, James and the other Beckwith children did lessons at the table and undoubtedly helped with chores such as gardening and laundry.

Wild game and fish provided food for the family, and boys learned to handle a rifle and fishing rod at a young age. They hunted and fished with their fathers. James probably preferred hunting to plucking weeds from the garden.

Each member of a frontier family had various chores to perform on a daily basis.

St. Charles was a surprisingly worldly place to grow up. In the past, both France and Spain had controlled the Missouri Territory, so people in St. Charles spoke French and Spanish. To keep pace with his neighbors, James learned both languages. The French and Spanish influence also affected the food, music, and art of the region.

The Beckwiths were among the early settlers who arrived in Missouri after the Louisiana Purchase in 1803. Pioneers took over Indian land, hunted game, and slaughtered herds of buffalo. Although the Beckwiths befriended local natives, some Indians resented white settlers and were hostile to the endless stream of wagon trains. Angry warriors raided and burned the settlers' homes, stole their horses, and sometimes even killed entire families.

To protect against such events, settlers joined together to build blockhouses near their log cabins. If Indians attacked, families could retreat to a blockhouse and defend themselves. Settlers stocked the blockhouses with food and weapons. When the alarm sounded, families hurried to the blockhouse for safety. During the most dangerous times, the alarms rang daily as Indians voiced their anger through raids on white settlements.

Contact between settlers and local Indian tribes frequently led to violence. One childhood memory stayed with James throughout his life. His father had asked him to take a sack of corn to the mill 2 miles (3.2 km) away. Young James happily agreed— particularly because he got to ride one of the farm's horses. Halfway to the mill, James stopped at a playmate's house to brag about being allowed to make the journey alone. When James shouted for his friend, no one came to the fence. James described the event:

Blockhouses were used by the military and on the frontier. Blockhouses were usually two stories tall and made of stone or timber. The second story would overhang the first with slits on the sides for gunfire. Tall fences often surrounded blockhouses, adding extra protection in case of attack.

> *What was my horror at discovering all the children, eight in number, from one to fourteen years of age, lying in various positions in the door-yard with their throats cut, their scalps torn off, and the warm life-blood still oozing from their gaping wounds!*

James returned home and told his father what he had found. Jennings Beckwith sounded the alarm throughout the settlement. The local men headed out in search of the Indians responsible for the slaughter. They returned a few days later with the scalps of 18 Indians tucked under their belts.

Life lessons were only a small part of James' education. Jennings Beckwith loved the life he had created for his family on the frontier but also recognized the value of formal schooling. He believed his children needed to read, write, and do arithmetic. The time came when lessons at home were not enough. When James was 10, his father sent him to school in St. Louis for four years.

At 14, James left school and served as an apprentice with a St. Louis blacksmith, George Casner. Work in a smithy was hot and demanding. Smiths made tools, weapons, pots and pans, and other household metal goods. They heated iron and steel over hot coals and pounded the metal into shape on an anvil. They fashioned horseshoes, nails, and hammers. A blacksmith earned a good living, but the work didn't offer the excitement that James craved.

In St. Louis, James heard travelers tell of their adventures in the West. By the time he was 19, he wanted adventures of his own. With dreams of the Wild West in his head, James was no longer content to be cooped up in a blacksmith's shop in St. Louis. He later said: "When I had attained my nineteenth year, my sense of importance had considerably expanded and, like many others of my age, I felt myself already quite a man." ❧

3 FREE MAN, MOUNTAIN MAN

cᴑᴋᴑ

Beckwourth and Casner got into a heated argument about Beckwourth staying out late at night and not doing his work. The truth was, Beckwourth fancied a young lady and had gone courting. During their conflict, Casner became violent and threw a hammer at Beckwourth. The argument ended with Beckwourth beating Casner and fleeing the shop. He hid at a friend's house and later boarded a boat headed for the Fever River (present-day Galena, Illinois) lead mines. Casner eventually caught up with young Beckwourth. As punishment, he returned him to his father in St. Charles.

At home in Missouri, Jennings Beckwith took legal action to free his son through a Deed of Emancipation. Although James had never been

By the time he was 19, Beckwourth found he was no longer content to work in a smithy.

treated as a slave, he still officially belonged to his father. Missouri had entered the Union in 1821 as a slave state. Jennings' actions in 1824 actually provided a safeguard for James. He could now legally leave Missouri without fear of being hunted down as a runaway slave.

While in Missouri, Beckwourth heard about General William Ashley and his partner, Andrew Henry, owners of the Rocky Mountain Fur Company. To recruit employees, the company placed ads in a St. Louis newspaper in 1822:

> *To Enterprising Young Men.*
>
> *The Subscriber wishes to engage ONE HUNDRED MEN, to ascend the river Missouri to it source, there to be employed for one, two or three years—For particulars, enquire of Major Andrew Henry, hear the Lead Mines, in the County of Washington, (who will ascend with, and command the party) or to the subscriber at St. Louis.*
> *—Wm H. Ashley.*

Beckwourth signed up and never looked back. At that time,

In 1822, Beckwourth joined an expedition headed for the same lead mines on the Fever River that had been part of his earlier escape route. In the end, he earned about $700 hunting for the group. He became friends with local Indians who showed him prime hunting grounds. During this time, Beckwourth improved his skills with an ax and bow and arrow, and he became a talented bareback rider. These abilities proved useful in his later life.

most fur-trading companies engaged in money-free business practices. Employees bartered, or traded goods, with local Indians for animal pelts. The men rarely did any actual trapping themselves and were paid between $200 and $400 once a year. The company covered the cost of newly constructed forts and trading posts and exchanged food, fabric, beads, blankets, alcohol, guns, and ammunition in return for furs from the Indians.

Beaver fur was especially valuable because it was used to make fashionable European hats. White traders also accepted buffalo hides and bear, fox, and otter fur. Every summer, the traders' employer

After reading William Ashley's ad in a St. Louis newspaper, Beckwourth eagerly embarked on his career as a fur trader.

Certain expressions and phrases were unique to America's mountain man culture:

buffalo chip—*dried buffalo manure used as fuel in fires*
buffalo cider—*fluid found around a buffalo's stomach; drunk by mountain men and Indians*
crimpy day—*a very cold day*
dumpling dust—*flour*
medicine—*the secret charms or magic of an Indian or tribe; bait for trapping*
mud hooks—*feet*
square—*a man of courage, honesty, and integrity*

collected the furs and replenished any supplies that were needed for the workers to continue bartering.

Ashley and Henry developed a new system in which their men worked as actual trappers in the Rocky Mountains. Instead of trading with Indians, employees independently hunted and trapped. The arrangement was simple. Trappers gave half of their fur pelts to Ashley and Henry and received whatever supplies they needed to reach the Rockies before winter began. The trappers then sold the other half of the furs and used the money to support themselves once the trapping season started.

The adventurers who joined Ashley and Henry became some of the country's greatest guides, explorers, and mountain men. Jim Bridger, a trapper for the Rocky Mountain Fur Company, later spotted Utah's Great Salt Lake. William Sublette eventually became the first white man to view the geysers at Yellowstone Park. Jedediah Smith became the first white explorer to travel overland to California through the

Southwest. He also found a pass through the Rockies that opened the way for thousands of pioneers to travel westward.

As a Rocky Mountain Fur Company employee, Beckwourth frequently faced grueling conditions— blizzards, bitter cold, ice storms, near starvation, and rushing spring rivers. Trappers often fended off bear attacks and prowling wolf packs.

As a trapper, Beckwourth faced a rough and rugged existence.

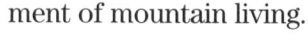

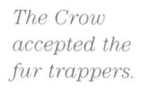

The Crow accepted the fur trappers.

Another danger lay in contact with certain Indian tribes. Local Indians proved either hostile or helpful. The Blackfoot were considered enemies, while the Crow were a friendlier people. The weather and wild animals also presented a potential danger. Beckwourth, however, relished the peril, the adventure, and excitement of mountain living.

The trappers wore buckskin shirts, leggings, and moccasins. They wrapped themselves in buffalo robes in order to brave the cold winters high in the mountains. They journeyed thousands of miles over land and across rivers, passing through areas that had previously never been seen by white men. The threat of hungry wolf packs, grizzly bears, and hostile Indians proved a constant challenge. They also provided plots for some rather engaging tall tales.

Beckwourth enjoyed spinning outrageous tales about his escapades: "The Indians were close at my heels; their bullets were whizzing past me; their yells sounded painfully in my ears; and I could almost feel the knife making a circuit around my skull." He became known throughout the mountains as a skilled liar. No doubt his adventures were less exciting in real life than the versions he told around the campfire.

The trappers worked in groups that were scattered across the Rockies. After months of isolation, they looked forward to attending a rendezvous, a meeting held during the summer months. To spread word of the first rendezvous, held in 1825, Ashley used a system called moccasin mail. This system involved leaving messages in trees, hollow logs, and under rocks. Messages were often placed in old moccasins so they would be easier to find. They frequently told about the conditions of the trails ahead or details concerning the summer rendezvous, such as the appointed place of meeting. Ashley used moccasin mail to convey the following message:

Mountain men claimed to be tough as nails, but few were tougher than Hugh Glass (1800?-1833). In September 1823, a bear mauled Glass. When his companions saw the wounds to his arms, legs, body, and neck, they left him for dead. Upon awakening, Glass realized he was alone and badly injured. He set his own broken leg and crawled about 100 miles (160 km) to the Cheyenne River, where he built a raft. Glass traveled by water for another 100 miles (160 km), finally reaching Fort Kiowa, located in present-day South Dakota. Glass lived on berries, roots, and the raw meat of a downed bison calf during the trip, which took him about six months.

The place of rendezvous for all our parties on or before the 10th July next and that the places be known—trees will be pealed standing the most conspicuous near the junction of the rivers or above the mountains as they may be. Should such a place be without timber I will raise a mound of earth five high or set up rocks the top of which will be made red with vermillion thirty feet distant from the same—one foot below the surface of the earth a northwest direction will be deposited a letter communicating to the party any thing that I may deem necessary.

Clearly, only experienced mountain men and guides were able to find their way to the meeting place. The rendezvous in 1825 became a tradition over the next 15 years, during the height of the fur trade. The annual gathering was an opportunity for mountain men, Indian trappers, and traders for the Rocky Mountain Fur Company to barter goods, play games, hold contests and races, and swap stories. Though the gathering changed location each summer, it was always held in a place that accommodated up to 500 trappers and 3,000 Indians.

Mountain men navigated rivers in bull boats and buffalo boats. Bull boats were small, bowl-shaped boats made of skins stretched over a willow frame. They were hard to control but easy to make. The larger buffalo boats were traditionally shaped like canoes and were made of buffalo skins.

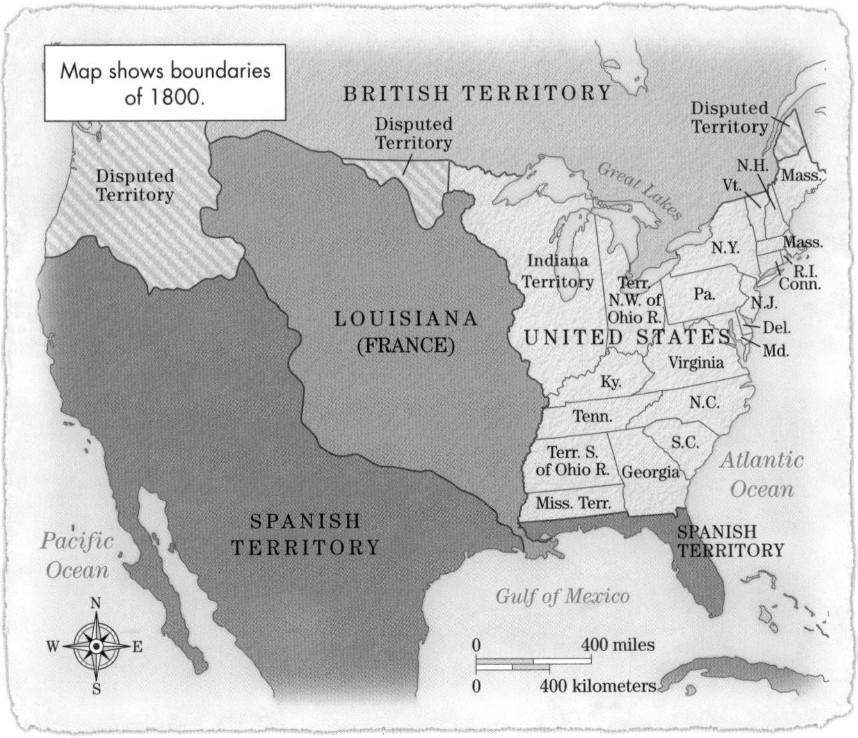

Map shows boundaries of 1800.

BRITISH TERRITORY

Disputed Territory

Disputed Territory

Disputed Territory

N.H.
Vt.
Mass.

Great Lakes

Indiana Territory

Terr. N.W. of Ohio R.

Pa.

N.Y.

Mass.
R.I.
Conn.
N.J.
Del.
Md.

LOUISIANA (FRANCE)

UNITED STATES

Virginia

Ky.

Tenn.

N.C.

Terr. S. of Ohio R.

Georgia

S.C.

Miss. Terr.

Atlantic Ocean

SPANISH TERRITORY

Pacific Ocean

SPANISH TERRITORY

Gulf of Mexico

N
W   E
S

0   400 miles
0   400 kilometers

The rendezvous was also a chance to purchase supplies such as flour, coffee, and salt. Women and children sometimes attended the yearly gathering, often described as a powwow and circus rolled into one. Beckwourth attended the festivities in 1825. It was there that he quickly earned his reputation as a "gaudy liar." ♔

During James Beckwourth's lifetime, the United States underwent a rapid expansion. When he was born, other nations still controlled vast territory in North America.

4 SPIN IT OUT IN THE FIRELIGHT

❧

James Beckwourth's talents as a storyteller were welcome at the 1825 rendezvous at Henry's Fork of the Green River in Wyoming. He was a powerful, engaging speaker with a hypnotizing voice. As historian Dale L. Morgan said, "To be a gifted liar was as much a part of mountain honor as hard drinking or straight shooting. ... The only sin is the sin of being dull."

Beckwourth used real life events and stretched the facts to build his image. The story never was that he caught and skinned 10 beavers in one day. Beckwourth claimed that the number was closer to 100 and that he accomplished this feat during a raging blizzard. He never covered 10 miles (16 km) on foot while being chased by a couple of Indian

A mountain man faced challenges and hazards most days of the year, so a tall tale was a pleasant escape from his harsh existence.

43

braves. No, Beckwourth ran 100 miles (160 km), barely ahead of 100 hostile warriors with arrows flying all about him. He never failed to paint himself the hero of every tale. He sometimes claimed to be present at two events that happened at the same time—held many miles apart. Perhaps Beckwourth was not an accurate historian, but most trappers who knew him agreed that he spun a whopping good yarn.

Beckwourth's skills as a frontiersman equaled those of his fellow mountain men. He handled knives, guns, rifles, and bows and arrows with remarkable accuracy. Beckwourth even looked the part of a dramatic mountain man—tall, muscular, rugged, and weatherworn. His thick dark hair fell to his waist and was braided in long rolls that were sometimes decorated with brightly colored ribbons. Earrings dangled from his multiple ear piercings, and he wore gold chains around his neck. Beckwourth looked like a pirate in buckskins.

Mountain men needed to be expert marksmen. The difference between a hit and a miss could mean survival or starvation. No mountain man could afford to waste ammunition or go hungry. Beckwourth typically bagged bear, buffalo, elk, antelope, and deer. The beasts provided skins for clothing or blankets and meat for several weeks. When necessary, he also shot small game such as

fox, rabbit, and muskrat. If meat was scarce, Beckwourth survived on dried berries, nuts, bark, bugs, and sometimes even leather.

Each trapper in a brigade was responsible for performing a certain task.

Trappers usually traveled in brigades of 40 to 60 people. Each man had specific duties within the brigade. Some tended camp, while others hunted game. Every brigade had its leader, and Beckwourth should have been an ideal candidate for the job. But he claimed that he refused leadership when it was offered to him:

The leadership of a party of a fur company is a very responsible post. Placed similarly to a captain of a whaling vessel, where all depends upon his success, if a captain is fortunate and returns from a profitable voyage, of course, in the eyes of the owners, he is a first-rate officer, and stands well for the future. But if he has experienced unusual hardships, and returns more or less unsuccessful, he is disgraced in his command, and is thrust aside for a more fortunate man. It is just similar with trappers in the mountains; whatever is their fortune, good or bad, the leader is the person on whom the praise or blame falls.

From a base camp, the men worked in parties of two or three. They trapped from autumn until bitter cold temperatures made it impossible to travel. In the winter camp, the men played cards, checkers, and dominos. Some sang songs and told stories long into the night. Others read or learned how to read. They slept in shelters made of animal skins stretched over poles, similar to Indian tepees.

Wintertime in the mountains could be tolerable or nearly unbearable, depending on the weather and the trappers' supply of meat. A mild winter allowed the men to hunt and fish regularly. But blizzards and ice storms kept trappers close to home. On occasion, bad weather prevented hunting for weeks, leaving the men near starvation. Remembering a terrible storm they faced one season, Beckwourth said:

> *There was no game to be procured and our only resource was the flesh of horses which died of starvation and exposure to the storm. It was not such nutritious food as our fat buffalo and venison (deer), but in our present circumstances it relished tolerably well. When the storm was expended we moved up the river, hoping to fall in with game. ... It was mid-winter and every thing around us bore a gloomy aspect. We were without provisions and we saw no means of obtaining any. ... At this crisis, six or seven Indians of the Pawnee Loup band came into our camp. ... They invited us to their lodges. ... The Indians spread a feast, which as they had promised, made all our hearts glad.*

As spring arrived, the massive yearly thaw began. Snow-blocked winter passes opened, leaving popular routes oozing with mud. Once ice-crusted rivers now flowed fast and free. Trappers once again laid their snares for beaver, lynx, and otter. The men journeyed through territory that later became Colorado, Montana, Utah, and Wyoming. By some estimates, 1,000 mountain men wandered the rugged Rocky Mountains during the height of the fur trading era.

The men traveled light, carrying rifles and traps. They stored ammunition, gunpowder, knives, flints to start fires, hatchets, and extra moccasins on mules or packhorses. Smoking tobacco and drinking whiskey helped pass the lonely weeks on the trail.

Pemmican was a favorite food among trappers since it was easy to carry and kept for a long time without spoiling. It was made from dried strips of buffalo meat. After drying, the meat was pounded into a paste and mixed with chokeberries or maple syrup. The mixture was then packed into a leather skin. Tallow, or melted fat, was poured over the mixture and allowed to cool. Pemmican could be eaten cold, but it was usually heated to melt the tallow. Occasionally, trappers made sweet sausage by filling cleaned buffalo intestines with meat, fat, and spices.

Beckwourth learned to set his traps in ponds, creeks, lakes, and swamps. He smeared the traps with castoreum, which is oil from beavers' glands. The familiar musky odor masked human scents and attracted the animals to the traps. When a beaver moving underwater stepped on the disc at the trap's center, the device snapped shut and pinned the animal underwater, where it would drown. Trappers regularly made rounds to collect the dead animals and reset their traps. To prepare the pelts for sale, skins had to be stretched between poles and rubbed with rough stones to remove any remaining fat and muscle. A poorly prepared skin took on a stench of rotted flesh, which lowered its value.

Mountain men such as Beckwourth typically lived a hand-to-mouth existence. They spent most of their money on supplies for the next expedition. Money that was left over disappeared at the rendezvous on gambling, whiskey, and trinkets. When Beckwourth worked as a trapper, he had no permanent home. Yet most frontiersmen loved the freedom

Mountain men used mules and packhorses to help carry supplies across the rugged Rockies.

Trappers made rounds to retrieve the beavers and other animals they caught in their traps.

of their lifestyle and the opportunity to experience the untouched wilderness.

While some Indians were wary of the pioneers, most were friendly and eager to trade beaver pelts for guns, ammunition, and alcohol. Many mountain men spent years with tribes such as the Sac, Blackfoot, or Crow. Life among these Indians was luxurious compared to the constant challenges of pioneering. Women prepared food, kept clothes clean, and built warm fires. On the trail, a mountain man had to do these chores for himself.

Some frontiersmen had Indian wives and

learned various Indian dialects. Beckwourth himself mastered some of these in addition to knowing Spanish and French. Frontiersmen who learned to communicate with different tribes sometimes later served as Indian agents for the government as settlers headed further and further West.

Each rendezvous drew its share of local Indians. The Crow who attended the 1828 rendezvous became fascinated with Beckwourth. This may have been because of their earlier experiences with trapper Edward Rose, who was part African-American and who later become a legendary Crow chief. Beckwourth had many of the same characteristics that made Rose so popular.

At the 1828 rendezvous, fur trapper and guide Caleb Greenwood told tall tales to visiting Crow. He entertained them with stories about Beckwourth's skills as a hunter, rider, and fighter.

Tired of being peppered with questions about Beckwourth, Greenwood lied to his Crow listeners. He said that the mountain man was actually an Indian, sold by the Cheyenne to the whites when he was just a child. The Crow rejoiced and insisted that Beckwourth return with them to live with their tribe.

At the time, Beckwourth and Greenwood laughed at the notion of his having Indian blood. Yet deep into the winter months of 1829, Beckwourth did, indeed, "return" to the Crow and live among them. ஒ

5 CROW WARRIOR AND CHIEF

ເໆໆໆ

The winter of 1829 didn't start smoothly for Beckwourth. While trapping with a group of men at the Powderhorn River, he got into a fistfight with a man who was offended by a lighthearted story Beckwourth told. Beckwourth also took out a loan from his employers for $275, which he promised to repay in beaver pelts. There was tension within Beckwourth's trapping group. In addition, he felt pressure to repay his debts.

In an effort to take care of business, Beckwourth joined a base camp where his close friend Jim Bridger was trapping. The two paired up for a day's work, but Beckwourth got separated from Bridger. Later that day, Bridger watched from atop a hill as a party of Indians surrounded Beckwourth and led their captive away. Bridger thought the Indians were the unfriendly Cheyenne and returned to the base camp convinced that his friend faced certain death.

But the Indians belonged to the Crow tribe. After hearing Greenwood's story at the 1828 summer rendezvous, the Crow were convinced that Beckwourth was a long lost relative. At the Crow camp, an old woman inspected Beckwourth. She said that her son, stolen by the Cheyenne as a lad, had a mole on his eyelid. She examined Beckwourth's eyelid, found a similar mole, and immediately declared that he was her long-lost son. As Beckwourth later explained, "The faithful fellows (mountain men) little thought that, while they were lamenting my untimely fall, I was being hugged and kissed to death by a whole lodge full of near and dear Crow relatives."

Mountain men who lived with the Indians enjoyed life within a tribal community and still trapped and traded. Beckwourth found that, with help from the Crow, he collected more pelts than ever before and turned a tidy

Today's Crow Indian tribe lives on a reservation in southeastern Montana, near Billings. Tribal enrollment is about 9,000 members. The tribe earns most of its income through coal, gas, and oil leases on more than 1.1 million acres (440,000 hectares) of land. Crow Indians also lease grazing and farming land. The tribe maintains active programs to improve housing, give children a good education, and promote health and wellness among the Crow.

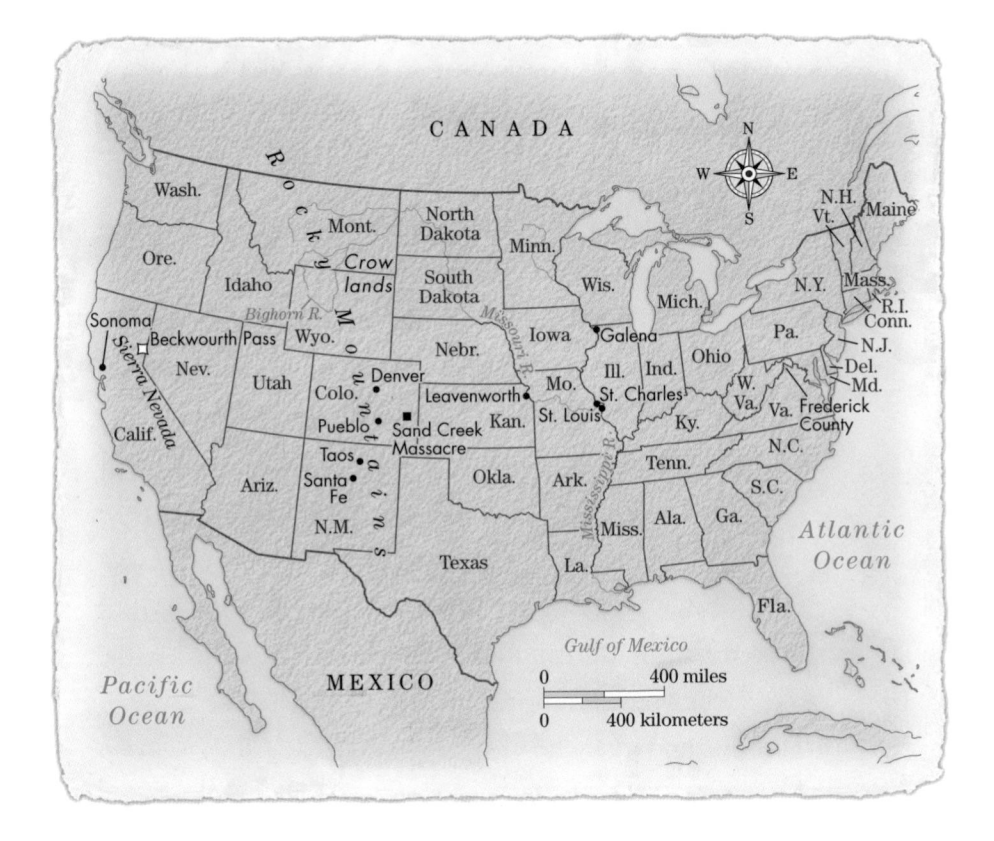

Beckwourth's career as a mountain man took him all over the rapidly expanding country.

profit from an autumn's work.

Beckwourth fit in well with his Crow hosts. Already an excellent horseman, he became even more skilled during his time among the Indians. He had no problem stealing horses, one of the Crow's favorite pastimes.

Since the Crow were known as great warriors, Beckwourth had to distinguish himself in battle. There were many ways a warrior showed his skill, but the greatest was in counting coup. This feat of bravery required the warrior to physically touch the enemy during battle. The touch could be made by hand or with a special stick.

Plains tribes respected the Crow for their skilled thieving. The Crow earned their reputation by stealing horses from other tribes and furs from white traders. Money held no interest for the Crow since they didn't have a monetary system of their own.

Stealing a horse was a rite of passage for a young Crow eager to become a warrior. Beckwourth led many raids where stealing horses was the party's primary goal. Among the Crow, Beckwourth was known as Enemy of Horses. He was also called Morning Star and Bloody Arm. As a warrior, Beckwourth returned victorious with scalps, prisoners, and many horses.

Shortly after joining the tribe, Beckwourth visited a trading post where he and several Crow started working for the American Fur Company, founded by John Jacob Astor. In 1833, Beckwourth led a band of Crow warriors in stealing horses, equipment, and furs from trappers who worked for his former employer, the Rocky Mountain Fur Company. The Crow traded the stolen furs to the American Fur Company. They used the horses and equipment to help them trap more animals.

According to Beckwourth's autobiography, he spent much of his time with the Crow fighting the

tribe's Indian enemies—the Cheyenne, Blackfoot, and Sioux. Beckwourth earned the name Bloody Arm for leading Crow warriors in a fierce battle against a Blackfoot war party.

For the Crow, a chief was a person of honor—not a single ruler. Most decisions were made by a group of tribal leaders called a council. The Crow had many war chiefs. Men who earned honors in battle by leading raids, counting coup, taking horses from a guarded corral, or stealing weapons in hand-to-hand combat became war chiefs. The title of chief guaranteed a certain amount of respect.

In his six to eight years with the Crow, Beckwourth distinguished himself and attained status as a war chief—possibly head chief of the entire tribe. As a war chief, Beckwourth sat among the tribal council and helped make the decisions that guided the tribe's actions.

Beckwourth enjoyed the Crow's nomadic existence and took several Crow wives. This was accepted behavior in Crow society. His wives took good care of him, cooking his meals and sewing his clothes. It has been suggested that he had as many as 10 wives at one time. In his autobiography, Beckwourth mentioned the birth of a single child—Black Panther (who was also called Little Jim). Other than a name, however, he offered no further details about his son's life.

The Crow spent most of their time hunting and warring against neighboring Indians. Beckwourth stayed with the tribe and made money from trapping and hunting. He also traded guns, ammunition, cloth, and beads for furs. For his services, he received a salary from the American Fur Company. Life among the Crow proved profitable for James Beckwourth.

As white settlers moved onto the Great Plains, they took land that had previously made up Sioux and Arapaho territories. Native people did not believe that they "owned" land. All land belonged to the Great Spirit. They used the land and hunted on it, but they did not have a title to it.

The increase in white settlers forced the Sioux

and Arapaho tribes into Crow territory. The Crow reacted. They formed war parties and terrorized the newcomers. Beckwourth grew weary of the constant fighting. Ironically, the American Fur Company fired him in 1836 because they held him responsible for the Crow's warlike ways and the negative impact on the fur trade.

As settlers pushed onto their lands, members of the Sioux and Arapaho tribes were forced onto Crow territory.

The true downfall of the American Fur Company did not come from the Crow but from silk top hats. Beaver hats were out; silk hats were in. The American fur industry ended as new fashion trends took over. Beckwourth lingered a bit longer among the Plains Indians, but he ultimately headed back to St. Louis. There was no future in fur trapping. 🐾

6 THE SEMINOLE WARS

⚬⚬⚬

Once in St. Louis, James Beckwourth had no work and nothing to keep him out of trouble. He started drinking heavily and began fighting. With the fur trade crashing to a halt, there were few jobs available for men like Beckwourth. He was running out of money and needed something to do.

Beckwourth's longtime friend, William Sublette, suggested a solution in 1837: join the Army and fight in the Seminole Wars. So Beckworth joined the war effort.

The United States had been fighting the Seminole tribe since 1816. The Seminole (a Creek word for "wild wanderer" or "runaway") were a band of Creek and other Indians who had left Georgia and the Carolinas and settled in Florida in the mid-1700s.

At the beginning of the 1800s, the Seminole were

Indians attacked an Army fort during the Seminole Wars.

joined by African slaves from the South who had escaped to Florida. Spain, which ruled Florida at the time, did not recognize Southern slaveholders' rights to their "property" and gave the escaped slaves land to cultivate. The escaped slaves, called maroons, sometimes married the relocated Seminole. The relationship between the escaped slaves and the Seminoles living in Florida was peaceful. The blacks who joined the Indians lived freely and paid a percentage of their crops to the tribe.

War broke out when angry Southerners, tired of losing slaves to Florida, demanded that the U.S. government do something. After negotiations with Spain

A Seminole village in Florida

failed, Congress authorized the use of force. U.S. Army troops attacked those living in abandoned Fort Nichols, killing 300 people—both blacks and Seminoles.

The survivors at Fort Nichols prepared for war. They stored crops, sent women and children deep into the woods, and bought guns and ammunition from traders. General Andrew Jackson led the Army against the Seminole forces in 1817. By May 1818, Jackson had captured the cities of Pensacola and Sewanee and asked President James Monroe for permission to end the war. Half of Jackson's soldiers had died from injuries, malaria, and yellow fever in Florida's swamplands. The Seminole forces suffered heavy losses, too, but no slaves were captured or forced to return to their previous owners.

The Seminole lived on valuable land. When Jackson became the governor of the new Florida Territory in 1821, he used a series

Most people remember Andrew Jackson (1767–1845) as the seventh president of the United States. Jackson originally gained fame as a military leader in both the War of 1812 and the Seminole Wars. He began his military career fighting in the American Revolution when he was just 14 years old. Jackson became a national hero when he led troops to victory against the British at the Battle of New Orleans during the War of 1812. He was so tough that his men gave him the nickname "Old Hickory." Jackson wanted all Indians moved west so that whites could claim Indian land. His Indian Removal Act led to the Trail of Tears, the forced march of thousands of Native Americans to barren land in Oklahoma.

When the U.S. Army presented a treaty to the Seminole in 1835, Osceola plunged his knife into the document in defiance. He had been born a Red Stick Creek and had joined the Seminole as a child. Osceola led his warriors through the swamps and backwaters of central Florida. Army officers tricked Osceola into meeting to discuss a truce in 1837. He arrived at Fort Moultrie, South Carolina, under a white flag of truce. The officers ignored the flag and put him in jail. Osceola caught malaria and died in prison

of treaties to push the Seminole farther south into the swamps. By 1830, Jackson had been elected president of the United States, and the U.S. government passed the Indian Removal Act. Jackson tried to use the new law to force the Seminole out of Florida completely. A few Seminole chiefs ultimately signed an agreement promising to leave Florida for the Indian Territory in Oklahoma within three years.

Under the leadership of Chief Osceola, however, some Seminole refused to honor this treaty. In 1835, the Second Seminole War began. The fighting continued into 1836 and 1837, with U.S. forces pinned down by the Indians. The natives knew the swamps and backwaters of Florida, but the U.S. Army did not. Soldiers wore wool uniforms that proved deadly in the Florida heat. The men suffered from swarms of mosquitoes, poisonous snakebites, and the ever-present, ferociously hungry alligators. Yellow fever and constant potshots by natives made duty in Florida even more deadly.

War costs money. As the expenses grew, Congress became impatient for an end to the fighting. But the U.S. forces could not defeat their enemy. The Seminole slipped away, moving deeper into the swamps, ready to attack another day. Missouri senator Thomas Hart Benton urged the government to form a brigade of volunteers from his state to go to Florida and solve the problem. Benton thought Missouri's mountain men—experienced trappers and Indian scouts—could help end the war.

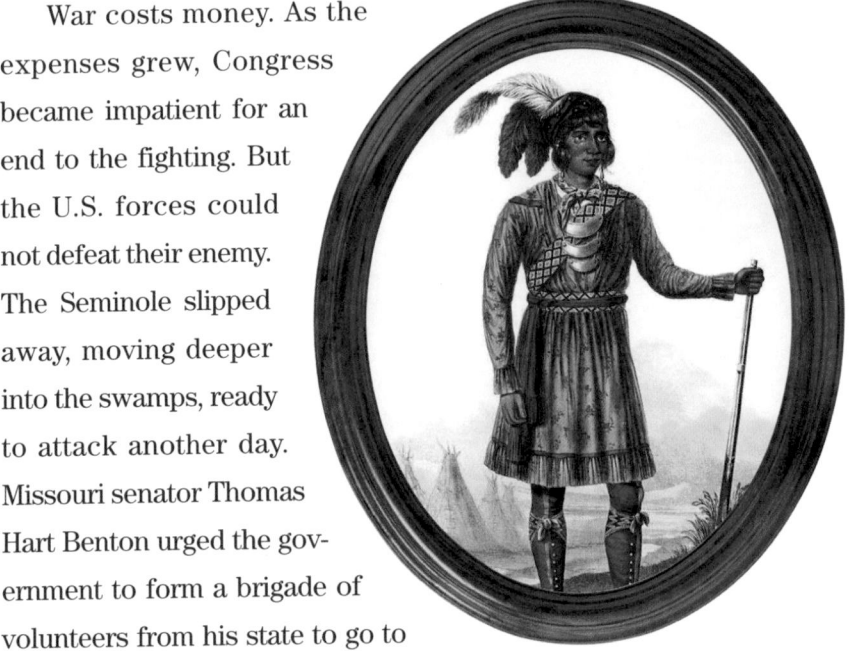

Chief Osceola resisted treaties that deprived the Seminole of their lands.

In 1837, James Beckwourth enlisted for a year and headed to Florida as a civilian employee of the Army. He was paid about $50 per month—more than most of the other employees and five times as much as the soldiers. His duties included serving as a wagon master and breaking in mules.

By December, the volunteers found themselves on the front line with the regular Army, now led by Colonel Zachary Taylor. Some accounts say Taylor intentionally let the civilian forces bear the brunt of the Battle of Okeechobee on December 25, 1837.

James Beckwourth later described the battle:

> On the morning of Christmas-day our camp was beleaguered by a large force of Indians, and Colonel Taylor ordered an advance upon them. ... As our line advanced ... many were singled out by the enemy, and we lost fearfully in killed and wounded. ... The country lost several valuable lives through this slight brush with the Indians.

After this battle, the civilian troops settled into a lazy routine. For a little more excitement, Beckwourth agreed to carry messages between U.S. forts. He often traveled alone across Indian territory. Although this was more interesting than sitting around in the Army camp, Beckwourth quickly tired of this job as well:

> *I was determined to return to the "home of the free and the land of the brave," for I felt that the mountains and the prairies of the Great West, although less attended with renown, at least would afford me more the substantial comforts of life, and suit my peculiar taste better than the service of Uncle Sam in Florida.*

The homesick trapper served 10 months of his one-year enlistment. He asked for a furlough for the remaining two months to return to St. Louis. Upon his return, Andrew Sublette (William's brother) and old friend Louis Vasquez convinced Beckwourth to try trading with the Indians of the southern Rockies. Beckwourth would be dealing with the Arapaho, Cheyenne, and Sioux—all enemies of his Crow friends. ✖

7 ONCE MORE A TRADER

❦

In the summer of 1838, Sublette, Vasquez, and Beckwourth took a steamboat to Independence, Missouri, where they loaded up with wagons, horses, and supplies. They traveled southwest toward the southern edge of the Rockies and New Mexico, land that was then governed by Mexico.

The party skirted Indian lands and potential danger. Each day, Beckwourth rose early and saddled up. He headed out to scout for raiding war parties that might swoop down and attack the traders. These Indians were unfamiliar to Beckwourth, and included the Kiowa, Comanche, and Jicarilla tribes.

In the desertlike conditions of the Southwest, Beckwourth suffered from sunstroke. He was not used to the burning heat of the southern Plains and

Beckwourth, Sublette, and Vasquez headed toward the southern section of the Rockies in a wagon train.

had too little water to avoid being ill. "We were at the time 20 miles [32 km] from water; I was burning with thirst, the heat was intolerable, and hostile Indians were before us. After incredible suffering we reached the river bank, and crossed the stream to an island, where I lay me down to die."

Vasquez came upon Beckwourth near death. He raced back to get medicine from the wagons, which were following two days behind them. When he returned, Beckwourth was barely alive. The sun-dazed trapper rode in a wagon for several days before his health returned. Beckwourth eventually recovered and was placed in charge of a fort that Vasquez had established near present-day Platteville, Colorado. Vasquez and his partners moved on to set up more trading posts along the southern Plains.

Back at the fort, Beckwourth wanted to trade with the Cheyenne Indians and sent several messengers to find them. When the messengers returned unsuccessful, Beckwourth looked for himself.

When Beckwourth finally arrived at a Cheyenne village, he saw rancher and fellow trader William Bent. He was stunned that Beckwourth would venture into Cheyenne territory. The Cheyenne had been fierce opponents of the Crow, and Beckwourth had met and killed many of them in battle. "You are certainly bereft of your senses," Bent remarked. "The Indians will make sausage-meat of you."

Beckwourth played up to the Cheyenne's warrior pride. He told them that he was a fugitive from the Crow and that he came to the greatest tribe to be killed because he did not want to be murdered by an "inferior tribe." Beckwourth took a chance that paid off.

Old Bark, an elderly warrior of the Cheyenne said to Beckwourth: "Warrior, we have seen you before; we know you. ... We know you are a great brave. You say you have killed many of our warriors; we know you do not lie. We like a great brave, and we will not kill you."

Vasquez and Sublette gave up their trading business in 1840. For a while, Beckwourth went to work

Beckwourth was eager to trade with Plains Indians, even if they belonged to tribes that were considered enemies of the Crow.

for the Bents. He traded in and around northern New Mexico and southern Colorado and opened his own store in Taos, New Mexico. There, he met and married Luisa Sandoval. Little is known about her other than that she went with Beckwourth to the Arkansas River in south-central Colorado Territory.

In 1842, Beckwourth built his own trading post in Colorado and was soon joined by 15 to 20 families. Cabins quickly sprang up in the area. "We all united our labors and constructed an adobe fort sixty yards square [48 square meters]. By the following spring we had grown into quite a little settlement and we gave it the name Pueblo."

It wasn't long before Beckwourth, restless again, said farewell to Luisa and left the little town of Pueblo in 1843. Accompanied by 15 men, he loaded horses from the Cheyenne and set out for California. Beckwourth arrived just in time to take part in the Bear Flag Rebellion.

At that time, Mexico ruled California. Fearing that all non-Mexicans would be ejected from California, a group of Americans protested. They called themselves the *Osos* (Spanish for "bears") and raised a homemade flag with a bear and star on it in a courtyard in Sonoma, California. Under the leadership of John C. Frémont, the Osos declared the creation of an independent California Republic in June 1846. Mexico was not pleased.

John C. Frémont (holding flag) during the Bear Flag Rebellion

When the Mexican War began in 1846, the U.S. Navy occupied key cities in California, including Sonoma. The Osos aided the American military effort. In his autobiography, Beckwourth claimed that his biggest contribution to the war effort occurred when he stole nearly 2,000 horses from Mexicans in Los Angeles and drove them to Colorado. His training among the Crow had paid off again.

The Mexican War was short-lived. The Treaty of Cahuenga, signed in January 1847, ended the fighting in California. The Treaty of Hidalgo officially

John Charles Frémont (1813–1890) was called the Pathmaker of the West. He explored the western United States during five expeditions in the mid-1800s. Frémont's wife, Jessie, helped him write lively reports about the West for readers in the East. He named the Great Basin in east-central Nevada and calculated the correct elevation of Utah's Great Salt Lake—4,200 feet (1,280 meters). A skilled mapmaker, he created accurate surveys of land that helped future pioneers find their way West.

ended the war in February 1848 and gave the United States control of Arizona and New Mexico.

Arriving back in Pueblo with the stolen horses, Beckwourth discovered that Luisa had married someone else after hearing false reports of his death. Marriage in the West was a loose affair without the legal ties that exist today. Finding himself single again, Beckwourth sold the horses and left Pueblo and Luisa behind. Luisa had a young daughter, but it is not known whether or not James Beckwourth was the child's father. Using his profits from the sale of the horses, he bought a hotel in Santa Fe, New Mexico.

Hotel management did not provide the excitement Beckwourth craved. Beckwourth decided to leave the hotel under his partner's management while he took a job carrying messages between military bases. Beckwourth rode across land where most of the Indians knew him. The trip between Santa Fe and Leavenworth, Kansas, took him three weeks—a challenging 700 miles (1,120 km) on horseback. Being a courier kept him busy, but, like

James Beckwourth

The discovery of gold in California attracted thousands of settlers hoping to find their fortunes.

previous jobs, it was temporary work for Beckwourth.

In 1848, however, California lured Beckwourth back. A miner had discovered gold at Sutter's Mill. The gold rush was on. Thousands of fortune hunters headed west to the gold fields. There was money to be made and adventure to be had in the hills of California. But unlike the thousands of miners, Beckwourth wasn't interested in finding gold—he simply wanted to deliver the mail. The former mountain man still liked traveling from place to place. ॐ

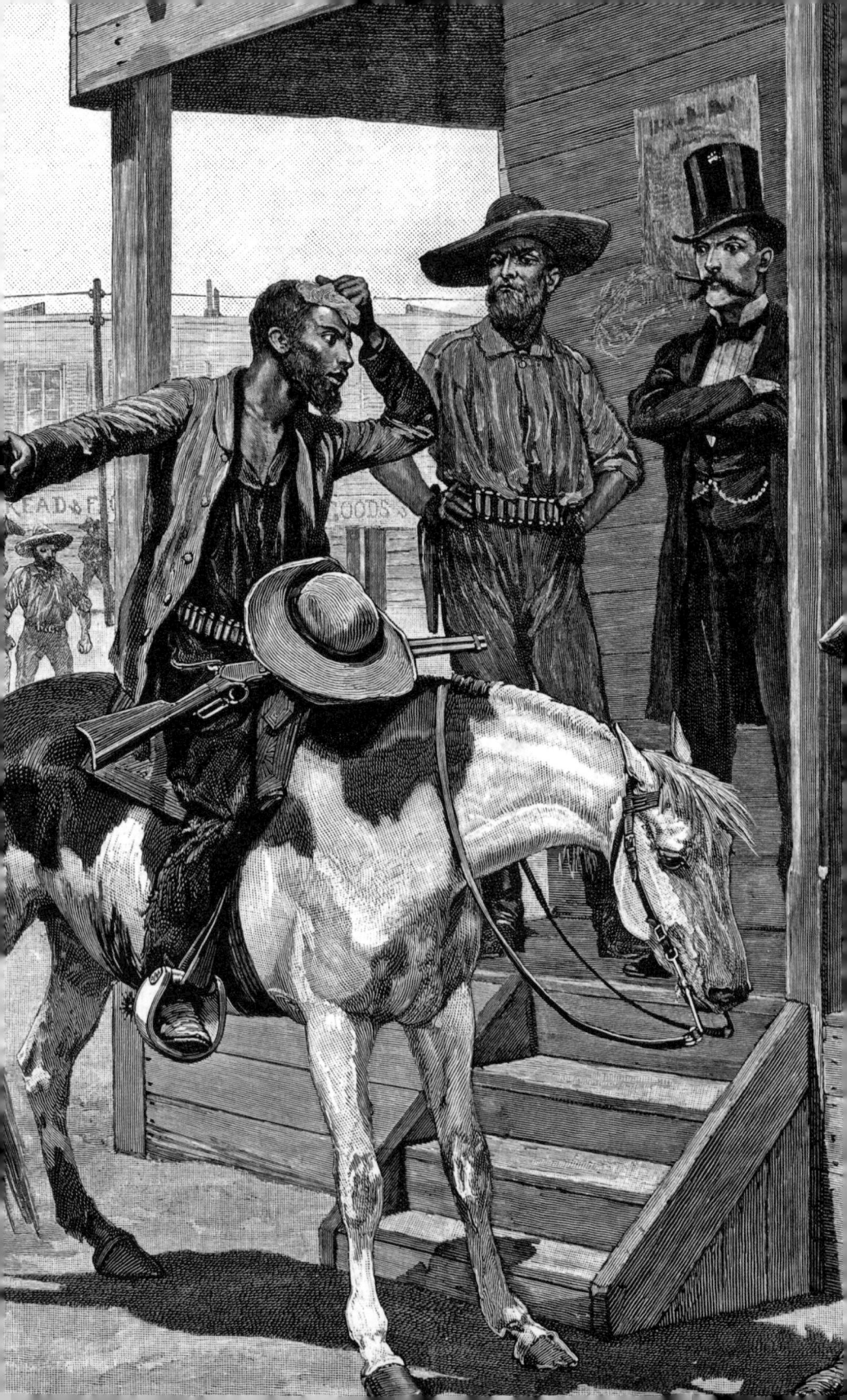

8 DISCOVERING THE BECKWOURTH PASS

❧

California's military authorities hired Beckwourth as a dispatch messenger. He and other couriers rode one of four stretches on the 500-mile (800-km) trip between San Diego and San Francisco.

On one such trip, Beckwourth encountered a horrid scene near Monterey. Dana's Ranch was a former mission and a common stopping point for Beckwourth along his route. It lay along the Salinas River and was run by the Reed family. When Beckwourth neared the mission, he was usually greeted by loud barking from the family dogs. On this evening, only the steady chirp of crickets met him.

Night was falling, but no lights burned in the mission's windows. Beckwourth entered and stumbled over a body. The room smelled like smoke.

A dispatch messenger in the West during the mid-1800s

Beckwourth returned to his horse and grabbed two loaded pistols. By the light of a hastily made torch, he discovered a trail of blood leading from the dead man toward the inner rooms of the mission. He quietly searched the other rooms, ready for an ambush at any moment. In a back room, he made a gruesome discovery. Several bodies lay stacked like pieces of firewood. Beckwourth ran from the mission. He mounted his horse and galloped straight to the military garrison at Monterey.

Beckwourth breathlessly described his discovery to Lieutenant William T. Sherman. The lieutenant sent soldiers to the mission. They followed the trail left by the murderers and captured them five days later. The murderers were either killed outright or hanged after being found guilty at trial.

Sherman and Beckwourth became friends. Although Beckwourth had a reputation of being a great liar, Sherman valued his reports of Plains events. Sherman later said, "Jim Beckwourth

William T. Sherman (1820–1891) gained fame as a Union general during the Civil War. As general commander of the Army during the 1870s, Sherman directed the attacks that forced Plains Indians onto reservations.

was, in my estimate, one of the best chroniclers of events on the plains that I have encountered."

Beckwourth resigned as a dispatch rider after only a few more months. He wandered from one California town to the next, playing cards, prospecting for gold, and stealing horses. His activities led him deep into the Sierra Nevada. In 1850, Beckwourth discovered a low pass over this mountain range. The pass would provide settlers with an easier journey into California.

With the help of the mayor of Marysville, California, Beckwourth worked on a road through the 5,212-foot (1,589-km)-high pass. The Marysville mayor assured Beckwourth that the city would pay for some of his development expenses. In August 1851, Beckwourth led his first wagon train over the newly completed road. Unfortunately, Marysville was damaged twice by fires, and the local government was burdened by other costs, making it impossible to pay Beckwourth. That first wagon train was the only one Beckwourth led through that year. He stopped acting as a guide when he realized that city officials couldn't pay him for his services.

The following spring, Beckwourth opened a hotel and trading post at his ranch in the lush green valley at the foot of the pass. He named the area Beckwourth Valley:

*My pleasant valley is 35 miles [56 km] at
its greatest breadth. It is irrigated by two
streams, with their various small tribu-
taries. ... All the streams abound with
trout, some of them weighing seven or
eight pounds. In the main one there are
plenty of otter. Antelopes and deer are to
be found the entire year. ... Grizzly bears
come and disappear again without ask-
ing leave of any man. There are wolves of
every species, together with
foxes, hares, rabbits, and
other animals.*

In late summer of 1851,
Beckwourth led the
first wagon train of
settlers along the
Beckwourth Pass to
Marysville. California.
Poet Ina Coolbrith
(1841–1928) was an
11-year-old girl on that
first wagon train. She
remembered being
swept up on
Beckwourth's horse
and riding bareback
into California.
Beckwourth, his hair
in long braids and tied
with colorful cords,
told Coolbrith and her
sister, "Here is
California, little girls,
here is your kingdom."

His small hotel was a welcome
sight to weary travelers in their
covered wagons. Beckwourth
replenished their supplies and let
their horses and oxen graze in
his pastures. By the time pioneers
reached Beckwourth's hotel, they
had traveled more than 1,000 miles
(1,600 km)—mostly on foot. They
had passed great seas of prairie
grasses, trekked over mountains,
and crossed deserts. They had gone
without baths and sometimes
without drinking water. They had
eaten beans and fry bread more
times than they could count.
Little wonder that Beckwourth's

hotel proved so attractive. A bath and clean bed, fresh food, and a chance to rest worn feet were more than welcome to travel-weary pioneers.

Settlers crossing the Sierra Nevada found Beckwourth's hotel a restful break from their exhausting trip.

In October 1854, Thomas D. Bonner arrived at Beckwourth's hotel. Bonner was a writer from the East Coast. He easily convinced Beckwourth that there was a lively market for true-life Western books. The two reached an agreement: Beckwourth would tell his tales, and Bonner would write them down. They partnered with Joseph L. Davis, who agreed to pay the publishing costs. The three men would share the profits from book sales. In the end, Beckwourth never saw a penny.

All through the winter, Beckwourth spun tale after tale. He probably slipped into the storytelling fashion of his mountain-man days. His tales featured epic heroism, gory deaths, and constant treachery on the trail. Bonner wrote it all down, struggling to spell the names of the people and places Beckwourth mentioned.

By the next summer, Bonner returned to Massachusetts. He and Beckwourth never saw each other again. In 1856, Harper Brothers published *The Life and Adventures of James P. Beckwourth, Mountaineer, Scout, Pioneer,* and *Chief of the Crow Nation.* Bonner had changed James Beckwith's name to Beckwourth—or perhaps it was just another spelling error on Bonner's part.

An image of Beckwourth used in his autobiography

The book gained Beckwourth public attention. People traveled to the ranch to meet the frontiersman, who by this time was nearly 60 years old. Scholars, however, blasted the book as being a "gory pack of lies." Beckwourth was despised by historians such as Francis Parkman, who wrote: "Jim Beckwourth, a mongrel of French, American, and Negro blood ... is a ruffian of the worst stamp, bloody and treacherous, without honor or honesty." Racial bias proved to be a common source of criticism against Beckwourth. Some people just couldn't stand a half-black man becoming a popular hero.

By 1858, Beckwourth had enough of ranching and headed back to Missouri. He never made it there and instead ended up in Colorado. Along the way, newspapers frequently announced his arrival in town. The now-famous Beckwourth was hailed as a great guide and interpreter.

At about this time, settlers were still swarming to the Western territories in search of land, gold, or freedom. These areas became involved in a tug-of-war over slavery. Southerners wanted the new territories and states to be slave states. Northerners opposed expanding slavery. The lifestyle of the Western frontier played a role in this debate. Pioneers faced harsh weather, backbreaking work, and threats from hostile Indians. The West was a place for equality. Men and women worked side-by-side as equals. The concept of slavery did not suit that sense of equality.

The edge of the frontier disappeared as the United States expanded from coast to coast. Construction of the transcontinental railroad was underway. Telegraph wires connected remote western towns to bustling East Coast cities. Having spent much of his life as a frontiersman, Beckwourth probably would have preferred if everyone moved back east of the Mississippi River.

In Denver, Beckwourth again worked as a trader with his friend Vasquez. Beckwourth became Vasquez's storekeeper and tried to settle down. He bought some property and, at the age of 60, married a young woman named Elizabeth Lettbetter. Beckwourth still stayed in touch with his Cheyenne

Denver at about the time Beckwourth settled there

friends who traded in Denver. During the Indians' visits, other settlers often treated the Cheyenne with hostility. Tension built between certain tribes and the whites. Indians lashed out as settlers cleared their land and slaughtered the buffalo. Beckwourth asked his newspaper friends to publish appeals to whites to treat the Indians better. These appeals fell on deaf ears.

City officials appointed Beckwourth as a temporary agent to help ease the conflicts between whites and Indians. It wasn't long, however, before Beckwourth took part in the mission that turned into a bloodbath for his Cheyenne friends. ♋

President Abraham Lincoln signed the Homestead Act in 1862. It provided settlers with 160 acres (64 hectares) of public land, based on their willingness to clear and live on the property. A race for the free land had settlers lined up for miles. The gun sounded, and the eager farmers headed out on horseback, wagon, or by foot. By the start of the 1900s, homesteaders had filed 600,000 claims, totaling 80 million acres (32 million hectares) of land.

9 THE SUNSET TRAIL

Chapter

⤳⤳⤳

Beckwourth soon became restless again. His personal life was filled with drama, but it was not the kind of adventure that satisfied him. He and Elizabeth had a daughter Julia, but the child died before she reached 2 years old. Soon after, Beckwourth killed an intruder who broke into his home. He faced trial for manslaughter but was found not guilty. His marriage to Elizabeth fell apart shortly after that, and he married a Crow woman named Sue.

In the fall of 1864, Beckwourth was again hired as a guide and interpreter for the Army—a job forced on him by threats. He served Colonel John M. Chivington. In truth, the colonel was little more than a bloodthirsty murderer who used his military standing to fulfill his desire to kill.

Colonel John M. Chivington

Denver is known as the Mile High City because it is located at exactly 5,280 feet (1,600 m), or 1 mile (1.6 km), above sea level. In 1864, Colorado was still a territory with Denver as a center for mining, finance, and cattle. In Beckwourth's day, Denver was a Wild West outpost on the edge of the Rocky Mountains. Gun-toting, hard-drinking cowboys and mountain men headed to Denver for a bath, a bed, and a sizzling steak dinner.

Shortly before Chivington hired Beckwourth, some families in outlying areas had been killed by the Cheyenne. Public sentiment against the Indians grew, and Chivington and his troops used the deaths to hunt Indians.

Not far from Denver, Cheyenne chief Black Kettle camped at Sand Creek with the Arapaho and other members of his tribe. Many of the braves had gone hunting, so those present were mostly women and children. The Cheyenne believed they were camped peacefully under the protection of soldiers at nearby Fort Lyon. They even flew white flags above their tepees as a sign of peace, and an American flag flew above the chief's tepee.

On the morning of November 29, 1864, Chivington and his forces attacked the unsuspecting Cheyenne and Arapaho camp. The Sand Creek Massacre joined the list of murderous acts committed by whites against the Indians. The troops slaughtered old men, women, and children. Black Kettle barely escaped with his life.

At first, Chivington was hailed as a hero. The *Rocky Mountain News* reported the event, praising the colonel and his men. The article declared the slaughter a success.

Chivington and his men savagely attacked helpless Cheyenne and Arapaho during the Sand Creek Massacre.

Among the brilliant feats of arms in Indian warfare, the recent campaign of our Colorado volunteers will stand in history with few rivals ... Just as the sun rose they dashed upon the enemy with yells that would put a Comanche army to blush ... It was estimated that between three and four hundred of the savages got away with their lives. Of the balance, there were neither wounded nor prisoners ... In no single battle in North America,

The Rocky Mountain News *was first published in 1859 and continues to serve the* Rocky Mountain *area today.* William Newton Byers, *who arrived in Colorado in 1858, founded the paper.* Byers *used his newspaper to encourage agriculture, finance a railroad, promote Colorado for statehood, and improve the community.* According to historian Jerome Smiley, "The appearance of the* Rocky Mountain News *in 1859 marked an epoch in affairs of the pioneer community. ... The paper preserved much of the primitive history of that eventful year. ... There wasn't a single event of major importance to the building of Colorado that did not have the name* Byers *attached to it."*

we believe, has so many Indians been slain. ... All acquitted themselves well, and Colorado soldiers have again covered themselves with glory.

Then the truth came out. Stories spread of how Chivington's troops had butchered unarmed women and children. Chivington arrested six of his men. People thought they would be charged with murder. But these six were actually soldiers who had refused to participate in the massacre, including one of Chivington's own friends—Captain Silas Soule. Despite the arrests, however, Chivington could not stop the truth from being told.

George Bent, who was camped with the Cheyenne, described what he witnessed that day:

> *We [a party of Cheyenne and Bent] now started up the stream bed,*

*following the main body of Indians and
with a whole company of cavalry close on
our heels shooting at us every foot of the
way. As we went along we passed many
Indians, men, women, and children, some
wounded, others dead, lying on the sand
and in the pools of water. ... The fight ...
was kept up until nearly sundown, when
at last the commanding officer called off
his men. ... As they went back, the soldiers
scalped the dead ... and cut up the bodies
in a manner that no Indian could equal.*

Bent went on to describe how the survivors traveled 10 miles (16 km) from camp and stopped for the night.

*It was very far and bitterly cold. Very few
of us had warm clothing, for we had been
driven out of our beds and had had no
time to dress. ... There was no wood to be
had, but the unwounded men and women
collected grass and made fires. ... It was
on the women and children that the brunt
of this terrible business fell. Over three-
fourths of the people killed in the battle
were women and children.*

U.S. Secretary of War Edwin Stanton ordered that the men Chivington arrested be released and began investigating the colonel's actions at Sand Creek. Two weeks after he was freed, Soule was shot in the back by a soldier named Charles Squires in

Denver. Some people believe men loyal to Chivington hired Squires to kill Soule. Although Soule never got an opportunity to speak before the military commission, Beckwourth did. He testified that the Cheyenne were friendly and that Chivington and his soldiers slaughtered them. He also said that he served as a guide because he feared he would be hanged if he didn't.

By the time Chivington was brought up on court-martial charges, he had left the military. No criminal charges were filed against him, but an Army judge publicly proclaimed that Sand Creek was a "cowardly and cold-blooded slaughter."

Desperate to make amends with his Cheyenne friends, Beckwourth searched for them in January 1865. He went to the lodge of Leg-in-the-Water, a Cheyenne chief, to convince the tribe to make peace with the white man:

> *I told him I had come to talk to him; call in your council. I told them I had come to persuade them to make peace with the whites, as they were as numerous as the leaves on the trees. ... [They said] "The white man has taken our country, killed all of our game; was not satisfied with that but killed our wives and children. Now, no peace."*

Beckwourth no longer had a place in Denver or

with the Cheyenne. He tried trapping again but had little success. For a short time, he worked as an Army scout at Fort Laramie, Wyoming. After that, he and Jim Bridger served as guides for Colonel Henry B. Carrington of Fort Kearny, Wyoming. As part of their duties, Beckwourth and Bridger visited bands of Crow in Wyoming and Montana.

Mountain man Jim Bridger (1804–1881)

In autumn 1866, James Beckwourth died among the Crow in south-central Montana. Stories swirled about the circumstances of his death. Some accounts said that the Crow poisoned Beckwourth when he would not agree to stay with them as their chief. Another story was that he mortally injured himself after falling from his horse during a buffalo hunt. Yet another theory was that he simply died of old age.

The diaries of Lieutenant George Templeton provide an account of Beckwourth's death. Templeton wrote about meeting Beckwourth in 1866 and accompanying him to talk to some Crow warriors. According to Templeton, Beckwourth complained one night that he had a premonition something bad was going to happen to him.

At the end of September 1866, Beckwourth and a friend set out for the nearest Crow village. The friend returned to the fort a month later, accompanied by an Indian escort. He explained to Templeton that Beckwourth felt ill the night they left. When they arrived at the Crow village, Beckwourth's nose was bleeding. Both men stayed in the lodge of a Crow Chief named The Iron Bull, where Beckwourth died. The Crow buried him on their land.

By the time he died at about age 66, Beckwourth was old by mountain-man standards. Mountain men had rough, demanding existences, and few lived very long.

Beckwourth was many things to many people— storyteller and liar, horse thief, guide, frontiersman, white, black, Crow by choice, trader, trapper, friend of the weary pioneer, adventurer, and chronicler of the mountain man's life. Historian William E. Connelley said this about Beckwourth in his autobiography:

> *Few men equaled James P. Beckwourth, and he lived in the age of great men. The West owes him a debt it would be hard to pay for leaving such a record of his adventures in the plains and mountains. This work will come to be one of the great authorities; not that all it contains can be*

relied upon, but that it is mainly true, and that is a record of a life spent in the great West, the record being made by the man himself.

Beckwourth had a lasting impact on the steady stream of pioneers eager to push their way westward.

While Beckwourth's book is full of misspelled names and gross exaggerations, most of the major events have been researched and verified by historians. His descriptions of life among the Crow give readers an understanding of that tribe not found anywhere else. James Pierson Beckwourth headed West when that region was a "howling wilderness." His adventures there ultimately helped clear the passage for thousands of American pioneers. ✑

BECKWOURTH'S LIFE

1810
Sent to school in St. Louis, Missouri

1808
Moves with his family to a farm near St. Charles, Missouri

C. 1800
Born in Frederick County, Virginia

1800

1801
Ultraviolet radiation is discovered

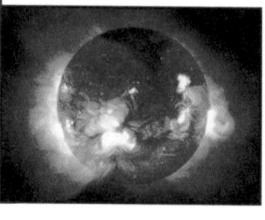

1809
Louis Braille of France, inventor of a writing system for the blind, is born

WORLD EVENTS

1814

Apprenticed to a blacksmith in St. Louis

C. 1822

Travels to Fever River (present-day Galena, Illinois) to work in lead mines there

CA. 1824

Joins the Rocky Mountain Fur Company as a trapper; father legally frees him from slavery

1820

1814–1815

European states meet in Vienna, Austria, to redraw national borders after the conclusion of the Napoleonic Wars

1823

Mexico becomes a republic

BECKWOURTH'S LIFE

1829

Joins the Crow tribe

1833

Begins work with the American Fur Company; is considered a chief by the Crow

1836

Fired by the American Fur Company

1835

1833

Great Britain abolishes slavery

1836

Texans defeat Mexican troops at San Jacinto after a deadly battle at the Alamo

WORLD EVENTS

1837

Works as a mule driver and messenger for the U.S. Army in Florida during the Second Seminole War

1838–42

Works as a trader in Colorado and New Mexico; opens a general store in Taos, New Mexico; marries Luisa Sandoval; helps found Pueblo, Colorado

1845

Leads trade expedition to California; participates in the Bear Flag Rebellion

1840

1840

Auguste Rodin, famous sculptor of *The Thinker*, is born

BECKWOURTH'S LIFE

1850–51

Builds the Beckwourth Trail in the Sierra Nevada; leads settlers through it and establishes ranch in Beckwourth Valley (Sierra Valley)

1854

Dictates his memoirs to T. D. Bonner

1858

Leaves California; settles in Denver as an Indian agent to the Cheyenne

1850

1855

1852

Postage stamps are widely used

1858

English scientist Charles Darwin presents his theory of evolution

WORLD EVENTS

1864

Is present at the Sand Creek Massacre; later testifies about the massacre before Congress

1866

Dies along the Bighorn River in south-central Montana while visiting the Crow during the fall

C. 1860

Marries Elizabeth Lettbetter

1865

1860

Austrian composer Gustav Mahler is born in Kalischt (now in Austria)

1865

Lewis Carroll writes *Alice's Adventures in Wonderland*

DATE OF BIRTH: About 1800

BIRTHPLACE: Frederick County, Virginia

FATHER: Jennings Beckwith (1762–1835)

MOTHER: A Beckwith slave

EDUCATION: Attended four years of school and apprenticed as a blacksmith; was fluent in French, Spanish, and many Indian dialects

FIRST SPOUSE: Luisa Sandoval

DATE OF MARRIAGE: About 1841

CHILDREN: Possibly a daughter

SECOND SPOUSE: Elizabeth Lettbetter

DATE OF MARRIAGE: About 1860

CHILDREN: Julia (1862–1864)

OTHER SPOUSES: Various Crow wives

CHILDREN: Black Panther (Little Jim)

DATE OF DEATH: End of September/beginning of October 1866

PLACE OF BURIAL: A Crow village, south-central Montana

In the Library

Altman, Susan R. *Extraordinary African Americans.* New York: Children's Press, 2001.

Collins, James L. *The Mountain Men.* New York: Franklin Watts, 1996.

Dolan, Sean. *James Beckwourth.* New York: Chelsea House Publishers, 1992.

Haskins, J. M. *Against All Opposition: Black Explorers in America.* New York: Walker & Co., 1992.

Monceaux, Morgan, and Ruth Katcher. *My Heroes, My People: African Americans and Native Americans in the West.* New York: Frances Foster Books, 1999.

Look for more Signature Lives books about this era:

Crazy Horse: *Sioux Warrior*

Geronimo: *Apache Warrior*

Sam Houston: *Texas Hero*

Bridget "Biddy" Mason: *From Slave to Businesswoman*

Zebulon Pike: *Explorer and Soldier*

Sarah Winnemucca: *Scout, Activist, and Teacher*

ON THE WEB

For more information on *James Beckwourth*, use FactHound to track down Web sites related to this book.

1. Go to *www.facthound.com*
2. Type in a search word related to this book or this book ID: 0756510007
3. Click on the *Fetch It* button.

FactHound will fetch the best Web sites for you.

HISTORIC SITES

Fort Vasquez Museum
13412 U.S. Highway 85
Platteville, CO 80651
970/785-2832
To visit an 1835 fur-trading fort founded by Louis Vasquez and Andrew Sublette

Museum of the Mountain Man
700 E. Hennick
Pinedale, WY 82941
877/686-6266
To view exhibits related to America's mountain men, as well as fur trading in the 1800s

agents
people who represent another person or
an organization

anvil
an iron block on which blacksmiths shape metal

apprentice
a person who works for and learns from a skilled
tradesperson for a certain amount of time

chroniclers
people who record historic events

dialects
words and pronunciations that are different from
what's considered the standard language in a
certain area

emancipation
liberation, freedom from slavery

furlough
time off from military duty

massacre
a mass killing

mutilated
cut up

prominent
important, well-known

smithies
blacksmiths' workshops

sunstroke
illness cause by overheating or too much
exposure to the sun

Chapter 1

Page 10, line 4: From *New Perspectives on the West: People,*
www.pbs.org/weta/thewest/people/a_c/chivington.htm.
Page 11, line 28: Dee Brown. *Bury My Heart at Wounded Knee.* New York:
Holt, Rinehart & Winston, 1970, pp. 86–87.
Page 13, line 6: Ibid., p. 88.
Page 14, line 11: Ibid., p. 90.
Page 16, line 20: Ibid., p. 94.

Chapter 2

Page 21, line 7: James P. Beckwourth. *The Life and Adventures of James P. Beckwourth, as told to Thomas D. Bonner.* Lincoln: University of Nebraska Press, 1972, p. 13.
Page 24, line 10: Ibid., pp. 13–14.
Page 25, line 6: Gerald S. Snyder. *In the Footsteps of Lewis and Clark.* Washington, D.C.: National Geographic Society, 1970, p. 36.
Page 25, line 19: *The Life and Adventures of James P. Beckwourth, as told to Thomas D. Bonner,* p. 14.
Page 27, line 10: Erick Bruun and Jay Crosby, eds. *Our National Archive: Key Documents, Opinions, Speeches, Letters, and Songs That Shaped Our Nation.* New York: Black Dog & Leventhal Publishers, Inc., 1999, p. 447.
Page 30, line 10: *The Life and Adventures of James P. Beckwourth, as told to Thomas D. Bonner,* pp. 15–16.
Page 31, line 20: Ibid., p. 18.

Chapter 3

Page 34, line 13: Sean Dolan. *James Beckwourth.* New York: Chelsea House Publishers, 1992, p. 40.
Page 38, line 28: *The Life and Adventures of James P. Beckwourth, as told to Thomas D. Bonner,* p. 124.
Page 40, line 1: Excerpt from William Ashley's diary,
www.pchswi.org/ppr/Rendezvous.htm#loc

Chapter 4

Page 43, line 5: Elinor Wilson. *Jim Beckwourth: Black Mountain Man and War Chief of the Crows.* Norman: University of Oklahoma Press, 1972, p. 6.
Page 46, line 1: *The Life and Adventures of James P. Beckwourth, as told to Thomas D. Bonner,* p. 61.
Page 47, line 4: Ibid., pp. 42–43.

Chapter 5

Page 54, line 15: *The Life and Adventures of James P. Beckwourth, as told to Thomas D. Bonner,* p. 152.

Chapter 6

Page 66, line 2: *Jim Beckwourth: Black Mountain Man and War Chief of the Crows*, p. 90.

Page 67, line 8: *The Life and Adventures of James P. Beckwourth, as told to Thomas D. Bonner*, p. 418.

Chapter 7

Page 70, line 1: *The Life and Adventures of James P. Beckwourth, as told to Thomas D. Bonner*, p. 422–423.

Page 70, line 26: Ibid., p. 428.

Page 71, line 8: Ibid., p. 428.

Page 72, line 9: Ibid., p. 464.

Chapter 8

Page 78, line 28: *Jim Beckwourth: Black Mountain Man and War Chief of the Crows*, p. 119.

Page 80, line 1: *The Life and Adventures of James P. Beckwourth, as told to Thomas D. Bonner*, pp. 526–527.

Page 83, line 1: *Jim Beckwourth: Black Mountain Man and War Chief of the Crows*, p. 5.

Chapter 9

Page 89, line 5: James D. Torr, ed. *Westward Expansion*. Farmington Hills, Mich.: Greenhaven Press, 2003, pp. 85–88.

Page 90, line 25: Ibid., pp. 90–91.

Page 91, line 16: Ibid., pp. 92–93.

Page 92, line 12: From *New Perspectives on the West: People*.

Page 92, line 19: *Jim Beckwourth: Black Mountain Man and War Chief of the Crows*, pp. 179–180.

Page 94, line 22: Ibid., p. 8.

Appiah, Anthony Kwame, and Henry Louis Gates Jr. *Africana.* New York: Basic Civitas Books, 1999.

Beckwourth, James P. *The Life and Adventures of James P. Beckwourth, as told to Thomas D. Bonner.* Lincoln: University of Nebraska Press, 1972.

Bruun, Erick, and Jay Crosby, eds. *Our National Archive: Key Documents, Opinions, Speeches, Letters, and Songs That Shaped Our Nation.* New York: Black Dog & Leventhal Publishers, Inc., 1999.

Brown, Dee. *Bury My Heart at Wounded Knee.* New York: Holt, Rinehart & Winston, 1970.

Crow, Joseph Medicine. Edited by Herman J. Viola. *From the Heart of the Crow Country.* The Library of the American Indian. New York: Orion Books, 1992.

Everett D. Graff Collection of Western Americana
Newberry Library
60 W. Walton St.
Chicago, IL 60610

A House Divided, online exhibit
http://www.digitalhistory.uh.edu

Kastor, Peter J. "Making Missouri American: A Crowded Frontier in the Age of Lewis and Clark," Chapter 1 in *Missouri Almanac*, pdf from the Missouri Secretary of State.

Martin, Michael. "Mountain Legend." *American History* 31, no. 4 (Sept./Oct. 1996): 36–42.

New Perspectives on the West: People
http://www.pbs.org/weta/thewest/people

Gold Rush! California's Untold Stories, online exhibit,
Oakland Museum of California, http://www.museumca.org/goldrush

Mountain Men, Malcolm Rosholt online archives
Portage County Historical Society, http://www.pchswi.org

"Story of James P. Beckwourth." *Harper's New Monthly Magazine* 13, no. 76 (September 1856): 455–472. Available at Cornell University Library, Making of America, http://cdl.library.cornell.edu/moa.

Snyder, Gerald S. *In the Footsteps of Lewis and Clark.* Washington, D.C.: National Geographic Society, 1970.

Taylor, Quintard. *In Search of the Racial Frontier: African Americans in the American West.* New York: W.W. Norton & Co., 1998.

Torr, James D., ed. *Westward Expansion.* Farmington Hills, Mich.: Greenhaven Press, 2003.

Trappers/Traders/Explorers, Utah State History Site,
http://historytogo.utah.gov/

Wilson, Elinor. *Jim Beckwourth: Black Mountain Man and War Chief of the Crows.* Norman: University of Oklahoma Press, 1972.

Susan R. Gregson has been writing for more than 22 years. She is the author of nearly 20 children's books. She also writes magazine and Internet articles, speeches, and technical reports. Her favorite part of writing books is the research. Sue lives in Minnesota with her husband, two young sons, a dog, nine fish, and the occasional toad in the sock drawer.

Image Credits